*blue whale*

# 1 They are gigantic!

Blue whales are one of the largest creatures that have ever lived on Earth. Powered by a heart the size of a small car, they are bigger than all of the dinosaurs except the sauropod.

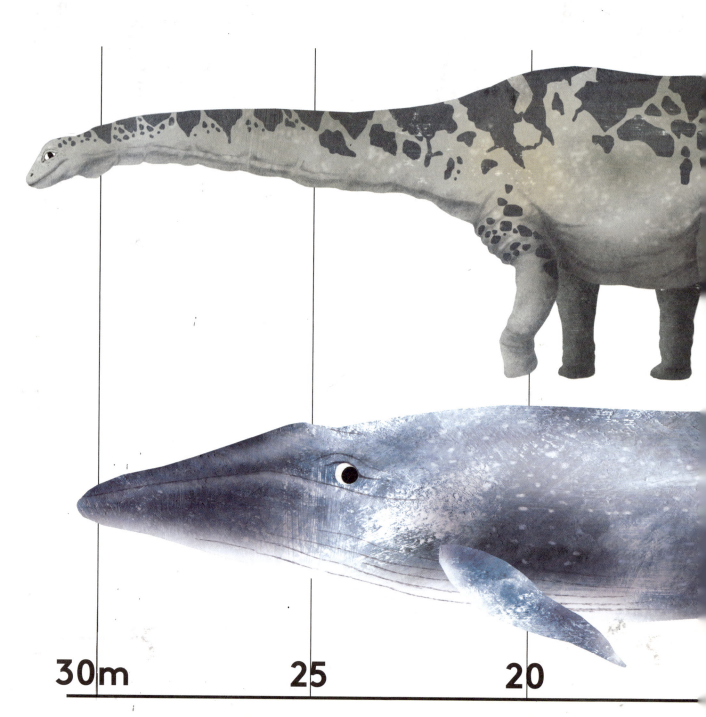

**30m**            **25**            **20**

Fully-grown blue whales are about 30 times heavier than an elephant – the biggest land animal alive today.

human

African elephant

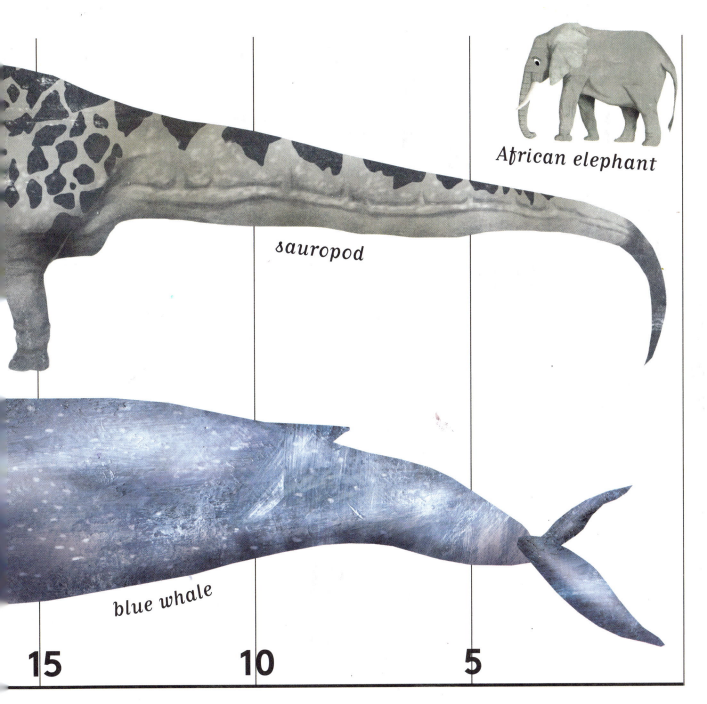

sauropod

blue whale

15    10    5

# 2 They are hard to find

Blue whales swim in deep water. They travel alone or in pairs across vast oceans, so these rare creatures are difficult to find.

*lagoon*

*octopus*

But if you head to the Canadian Arctic or stare across the warm waters of Baja California, a tropical Mexican lagoon, you might be lucky enough to spot a blue whale.

SHOW YOU LOVE A WHALE

See one close up in a museum! Natural history museums around the world have blue whale skeletons on display.

blue whale

seabed

starfish

# 3 They have yellow bellies

From above, blue whales look bright blue. But when they break the surface to breathe, their skin is grey. It is smoother than most other whales' skin. Blue whales swim too fast for crusty barnacles to cling on.

sunfish

sea turtle

But one plant does stick to its slippery skin. In cold waters, tiny yellow algae grow on the bellies of blue whales. This makes their bellies look yellow.

blue whale

algae

# 4 They sing across the oceans

Blue whales sing to keep in touch with each other when they are hundreds of miles apart. Their strange songs echo around the world's deepest oceans.

*school of tuna fish*

blue whale

The low moans of blue whales are the loudest sounds on Earth. But some are too low for human ears, so we only hear parts of their haunting underwater melodies.

# 5 They spout towering fountains

The easiest way to find a blue whale is to spot it blowing. A whale is a mammal, so it needs air to survive. When blue whales come up to breathe, they blow out a tall fountain of air and water.

*humpback whale*

*spray*

**SHOW YOU LOVE A WHALE**

*Go whale watching! Join a responsible whale watching tour to be amazed by blue whales.*

This spray spouts from two holes on top of the whale's head. When it dives again, after taking a breath, flaps of skin cover these holes so its lungs don't fill with water.

seagull

blue whale

blowhole

# 6 They have a giant mouth

When the blue whale eats, long pleats of skin under its throat unfold to create the world's biggest mouth. This expanding cavern leads into a surprisingly narrow throat.

gannets

blue whale

sardines

Flopping inside its mouth, the blue whale's tongue is as heavy as an elephant. Instead of teeth, it has rows of sieve-like bristles made from the same material as human hair and nails.

expanded mouth

# 7 They eat pink food

Blue whales feed on krill – tiny pink shrimps no bigger than a paperclip that live in gigantic swarms in the ocean.

blue whale

Nobody knows how blue whales find krill. But when they do, they gulp them in swirling mouthfuls of seawater. The shrimps get stuck between the whale's bristles and with its huge tongue, it pushes the water out and licks off the krill.

*krill cloud*

*deep water*

# ⑧ They are globetrotters

Blue whales travel to cold polar waters to find food. In these icy seas they eat 40 million krill every day. They fatten up to survive for months in warmer seas where food is scarce.

Canadian Arctic

NORTH AMERICA

Baja California

Equator

SOUTH AMERICA

SHOW YOU LOVE A WHALE

Help stop climate change! Warming seas are one of the reasons why krill is disappearing.

Blue whales migrate to the equator where they breed and the females give birth. Months later they return to colder seas with their newborn calves to feed.

EUROPE

ASIA

AFRICA

OCEANIA

Equator

# **9** They are mighty mothers

Blue whales give birth to the biggest babies in the world. Born tail first in warm waters, newborn calves grow quickly on their mother's rich milk. This helps them keep up and stay close as she swims.

ice

blue whale calf

Sometimes a whale mother bumps her baby to the surface to help it rest and breathe. She keeps her calf close to protect it from killer whales – the blue whale's only predator.

killer whale

blue whale

# 10 They are survivors

Once, the seas teemed with blue whales. But hundreds of thousands were hunted for meat and blubber, so they almost disappeared. Whaling is now banned, but blue whales are still in danger of extinction.

fishing boat

dolphins

seal